Children's Torah

Activity Book 4

By Belinda McCallion

LANG
BOOK PUBLISHING

langbookpublishing.com

National Library of New Zealand Cataloguing-in-Publication Data.

Lang Book Publishing 2018.

ISBN 978-0-9951045-1-8

Published in New Zealand.
A catalogue record for this book is available from the National Library of New Zealand.
Kei te pātengi raraunga o Te Puna Mātauranga o Aotearoa te whakarārangi o tēnei pukapuka.

This book Belongs to:

_____

How to use this book:

These worksheets have been especially designed for easy photocopy duplication.

Each lesson has 3 parts; a Torah, a Haftara and a B'rit Hadashah.

The main page of each part is the instruction page. This is not intended to replace the actual reading of the portion but to be a tool that can be used to summarise the readings and find a few key messages from the readings.

The activity page relates to the lesson and is intended to be used to reinforce the messages. This page caters to a wide age group, as there is always a picture to colour and a more difficult activity. Each activity sheet ranges in difficulty level dependant on the lesson. There is an answer page at the back of the book if you get stuck.

Table of Contents

Parasha 34

Memory Verse

"Take a census of the entire assembly of the people of Isra'el, by clan and families."

Numbers 1:2 CJB

פרשת במדבר Bamidbar (In the desert) Numbers 1:1-4:20

STORY SUMMARY

ADONAI Tells Moshe to Count the People: First the leaders are chosen. Then, the males who are over 20 and can be soldiers, are counted. This does not include those from the tribe of Levi, because they are to serve in the tabernacle. Next, the camp position for each tribe around the tabernacle is given. Then, the Levites and the firstborn are counted, and money is paid for the difference. Following this, more instructions are given to the priests.

WORD FOCUS— THOSE WHO WERE CALLED BY NAME

Elitzur: G-d of the Rock

Nachshon: Tribal Leader

Eliav: ADONAI is Father

Gamli'el: Reward of ADONAI

Achi'ezer: My Brother is Help

Elyasaf: ADONAI has Added

Shlumi'el: Peace of ADONAI

N'tan'el: Given of ADONAI

Elishama: ADONAI has Heard

Avidan: My Father is Judge

Pag'I'el: Occurance of ADONAI

Achira: My brother is Evil

MAIN MESSAGE

ADONAI was bringing order and structure to His system. He was preparing His people to serve Him and to be a light to the world. ADONAI leads us into all kinds of situations that we might not understand, but often when we look back we can see something we learned. Then we can share it with others to bless them. ADONAI calls each one of us by our name, for the purpose in which we were created.

G-D of ORDER   **OBEY**   **BE SET APART**

Promise

Numbers 1:17 CJB

"So Moshe took these men who had been designated by name."

Did You Know?

When the census was taken there were over six hundred thousand men counted. That was the size of their army.

Bamidbar Numbers 1:1-4:20 Activity Sheet

Many have tried to know the colours and symbols of the tribes but not everyone has the same answer. Here is one interpretation (see answers page for reference information.)

Colour these flags the right colours and/or draw the symbol that represents each tribe of Isra'el.

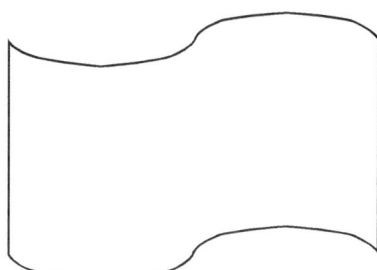

Name: Reuben
Colour: Red
Symbol: Mandrake (plant)

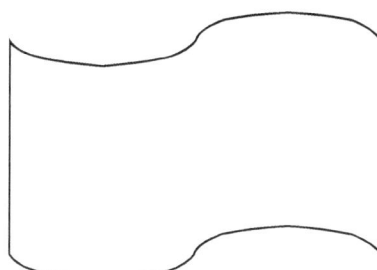

Name: Simeon
Colour: Green
Symbol: city (Shechem)

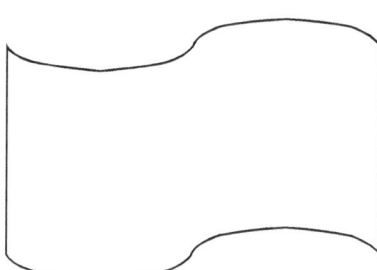

Name: Levi
Colour: White, black, red
Symbol: Priest's Breastplate

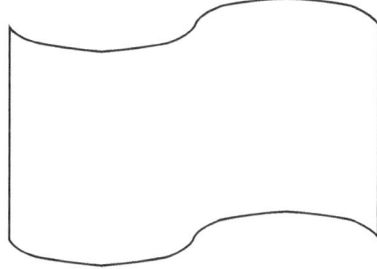

Name: Judah
Colour: Sky Blue
Symbol: Lion

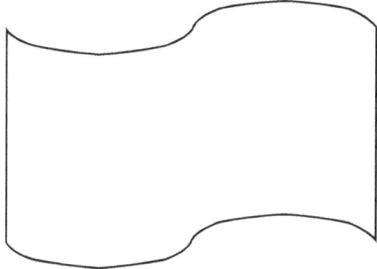

Name: Issachar
Colour: Dark Blue
Symbol: Sun and Moon

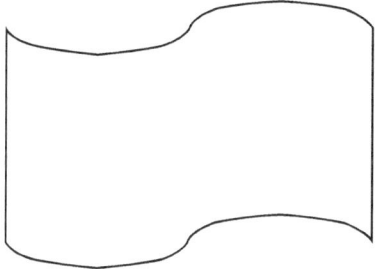

Name: Zebulon
Colour: Light Yellow
Symbol: Ship

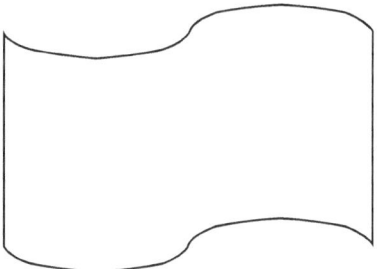

Name: Dan
Colour: Sapphire Blue
Symbol: Snake

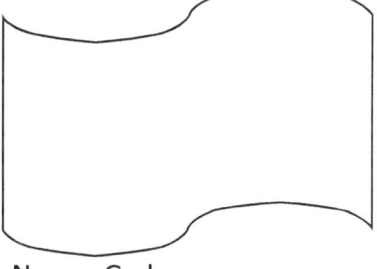

Name: Gad
Colour: Gray
Symbol: Military Camp

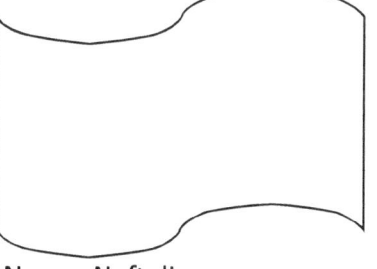

Name: Naftali
Colour: Pink
Symbol: Deer

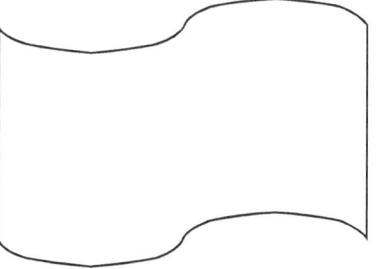

Joseph: Black, 2 Men

Ephraim: Black., Ox

Manasseh: Black, Oryx (large horned antelope)

Name: Asher
Colour: Pale Green
Symbol: Olive Tree

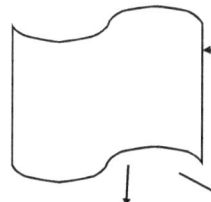

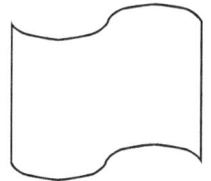

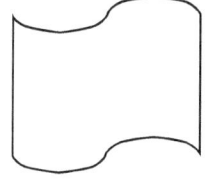

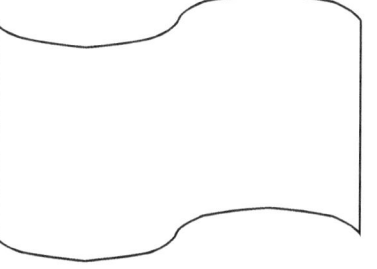

Name: Benjamin
Colour: Mix of all the others
Symbol: Wolf

Hoshea

Hosea 2:1-22

Haftara 34 (Prophets)

Memory Verse

"..Instead of being told 'you are not my people,' it will be said to them, 'you are the children of the living G-d.'"
Hosea 2:1 CJB

Did You Know?

Hosea was a prophet to the Northern Kingdom of Isra'el. This was the kingdom that was scattered.

Promise

Hosea 2:1 CJB

"Nevertheless, the people of Isra'el will number as many as the grains of sand by the sea, which cannot be measured or counted..."

STORY SUMMARY

Rejection and New Hope Given: ADONAI tells of a time to come when the people will be so many, they will not be able to be counted. At this time they will be accepted again. He is not going to overlook their rebellion, but He will turn their hearts back to Him so they choose to serve Him. Then He will bless and 'aras' (want to marry) them again.

WORD FOCUS

Aras: 'To speak for', 'to become engaged.' This is a perfect picture of what Yeshua has done and is doing. He speaks on our behalf and invites us to be His again. We are waiting and preparing for the 'wedding' day.

MAIN MESSAGE

In the parasha reading we saw the start of the plan, where ADONAI was preparing an army. In this passage we see the end, where war is over, and nobody needs to fight anymore. There will be peace and safety. Everything has its time. If you are going through a hard time, be encouraged that if you stay connected with ADONAI, times of peace will come. Don't give up.

WARNING   HOPE   PROMISE

PARENTAL NOTE: Discretion advised when using biblical narrative.

4

Hoshea 2:1-22 Activity Sheet

Peace

"When that day comes, I will make a covenant for them with the wild animals, the birds in the air and the creeping things of the earth." Hosea 2:20 CJB

Blessings and Curses

Help these children walk in the path of blessings. Stay on the path of blessings (B) and avoid curses (C). The paths will join up. You can go up, down, left or right but not diagonal.

C	C	B	B	B	B	B	B	B
B	B	C	C	C	C	C	C	C
B	B	B	B	C	B	C	B	C
C	C	C	B	C	B	C	C	C
C	C	B	C	C	B	C	C	C
C	C	B	B	C	B	B	C	C
C	B	C	C	C	C	B	B	B
C	B	C	B	C	C	B	C	C
B	C	B	B	C	C	C	B	B

Luke
3:22-28

B'rit Hadashah 34
(Newer Testament)

MAIN MESSAGE

Family lines were very important to the Jewish people. The parasha outlines the counting of the people, and the haftara presents a promise of increase. Here, Luke shows how Yeshua, through His blood line is the seed of G-d, Abraham and David and from the tribe of Judah. This gives Him authority be the promised Messiah.

PROMISE

"The scepter shall not depart from Judah, nor a lawgiver from between his feet, until Shiloh shall come: and to him shall be the gathering of the people."

Genesis 49:10 WBT

DID YOU KNOW?

Luke has a different explanation of the family line than Matthew. Many say one shows the mother's line and the other shows the father's line.

STORY SUMMARY

Genealogy Of Yeshua: Luke lists the family line of Yeshua from G-d to Adam through to Yeshua.

WORD FOCUS

Shiloh: 'The sent', 'the seed', 'the peaceable or prosperous one', 'the Messiah'. In all other places, apart from Genesis 49:10, Shiloh is a place name.

MEMORY VERSE

"The *Ruach HaKodesh* came down on Him in physical form like a dove; and a voice came from Heaven, 'You are My son, whom I love: I am well pleased with You...'" Luke 3:22 CJB

Luke 3:22-28 Activity Sheet

Family Tree

Choose one set of your grandparents. Draw and name the people in your family tree line from your grandparents down to you.

Grandfather:

Grandmother:

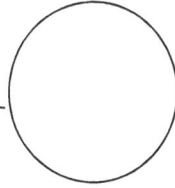

Mother/Father:

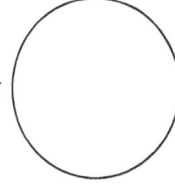

Me:

Family

"I will make your descendants as numerous as the stars in the sky, I will give all these lands to your descendants, and by your descendants all the nations of the earth will bless themselves."

Genesis 26:4

Parasha 35

נשא Naso נשא

(Take) Numbers 4:21-7:89

Promise

Numbers 6:24 CJB

"May *ADONAI* bless you and keep you.

May *ADONAI* make His face shine upon you and show you His favour.

May *ADONAI* lift up His face towards you and give you peace."

Memory Verse

"According to *ADONAI'S* order they were appointed by Moshe, each one to his specific service of work."

Numbers 4:49 CJB

Did You Know?

People took Nazir vows for different reasons. Sometimes it was to ask *ADONAI* for children if they didn't have any.

STORY SUMMARY

Tabernacle Servants Counted: Those dedicated for tabernacle service are counted, and duties outlined. Also, the donations of clans for the tabernacle are stated.

Guilt Ceremony: A ceremony that decides the guilt of a wife is explained.

Nazir Vow: The Nazir vow is outlined, and the blessing of the people is given.

WORD FOCUS

Nazir: Nazarite, meaning 'to consecrate', 'to separate'. This Nazir vow was made by those wanting to dedicate themselves fully to Adonai, and separate themselves from others.

MAIN MESSAGE

Adonai was separating a people unto Himself. The people were to be different than the world. The closer one came to Adonai, the more restrictions there were on him/her to be different, set apart and holy. As believers, we want to be 'counted' as His also. The closer we get to Adonai, the more like Him and less like the world we should become.

RELATIONSHIP   OBEY   BE SET APART

Naso Numbers 4:21-7:89 Activity Sheet

Long Hair

"Throughout the period of his vow as a *Nazir*, he is not to shave his head. Until the end of the time for which he has consecrated himself to *ADONAI*, he is to be holy; he is to let the hair on his head grow long." Numbers 6:5 CJB

Nazir Vow

Complete the crossword using Numbers 6:1-7.

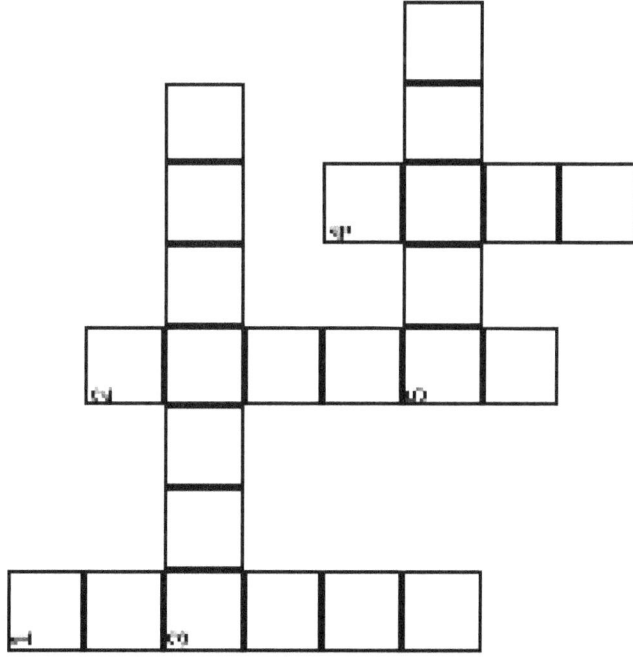

ACROSS

3. The Nazir was not to drink _____

5. The Nazir was not to _____ his head

DOWN

1. The Nazir was not to eat _____

2. The Nazir was not to touch a _____

4. The Nazir was not to cut his _____

Shof'tim

Judges 35

Promise

Judges 13:5 CJB

"No razor is to touch his head, because the child will be a *nazir* for God from the womb. Moreover, he will begin to rescue Israel from the power of the P'lishtim (Philistines)."

STORY SUMMARY

Manoach and His Wife Promised a Child: The wife of Manoach has not been able to have children. The angel of Adonai visits her and says she will have a son. However, this baby is to be a nazir, and help rescue Israel from the Philistines. She is not allowed to have anything from the grape vine or any other alcohol. She is also not to eat unclean food or cut the child's hair. When the baby is born, he is called Shimshon (Samson).

WORD FOCUS

Shimshon: 'Man of the sun'. The sun was symbolic of Adonai's glory. However, the sun was not always pleasant. Without protection, the sun brings death.

Main Message

If we read on about Shimshon we see that he ended up falling for temptation despite being set apart to be holy and being especially blessed. Maybe Shimshon began to trust in his own strength instead of Adonai's provisions. Let us never forget where our strength comes from.

WARNING   TRUST   HUMILITY

Haftara 35 (Prophets)

Memory Verse

"...Be careful not to drink any wine or other intoxicating liquor, and don't eat anything unclean."

Judges 13:4 CJB

Did You Know?

Shimshon was famous for his strength. Think how strong he must have been to carry away a large city gate, as shown in our picture on the activity page.

Shof'tim (Judges) 13:2-25 Activity Sheet

Shimshon

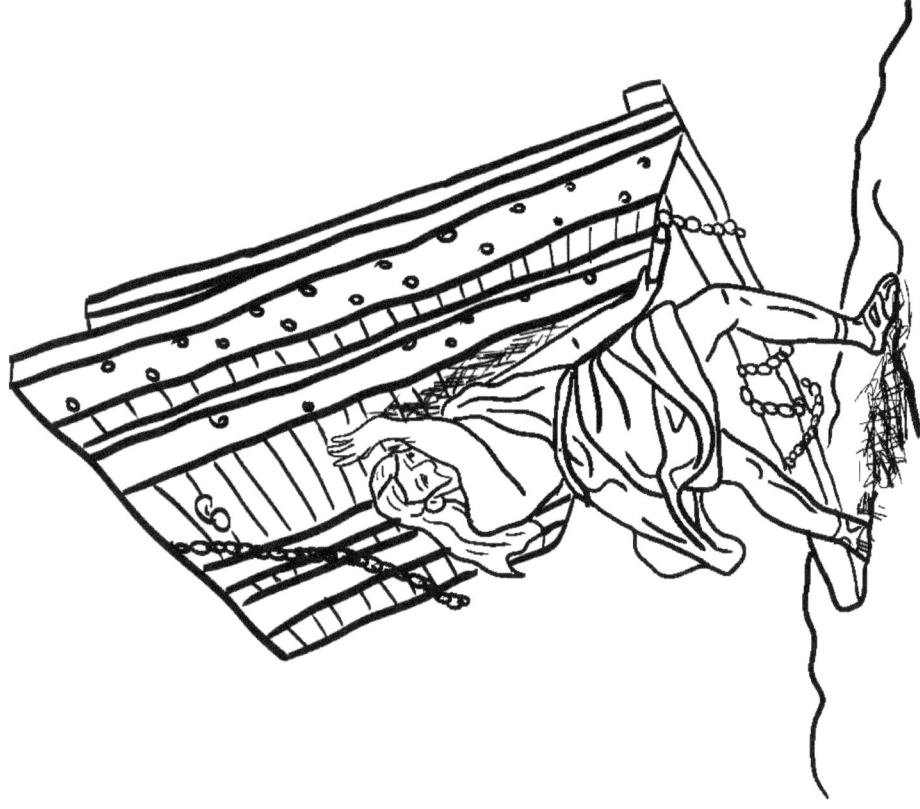

"Shimshon...took hold of the doors of the city gate, and the two posts as well, pulled them up bar and all, hoisted them on his shoulders, and carried them up to the top of the hill overlooking Hevron."
Judges 16:3 CJB

Source of Strength

Draw a separating line between these words to reveal the secret of Shimshon's strength. The first one is done for you.

THE|SOURCEOFSH

IMSHON'SSTRENG

THWASINHISHAIR.

IFHISHAIRWASTOB

ECUTHEWOULDLO

SEHISSTRENGTH.

Matthew
5:27-28

B'rit Hadashah 35
(Newer Testament)

MAIN MESSAGE

The parasha spoke of the ritual for jealousy. Here Yeshua is setting another standard before jealousy even has cause to grow. This is called a 'guard rail' or a 'fence'. Jealousy is ugly if it is allowed to grow. It makes us feel bitter inside. There are all kinds of things we can become jealous of such as our siblings or our classmates. Choosing to love our enemies is a guard rail for jealousy.

STORY SUMMARY

Yeshua Sets a New Stadard: Yeshua tells His followers that even looking at a woman the wrong way is sin.

PROMISE

"Love your enemies! Pray for those who persecute you! Then you will become children of your Father in Heaven."

Matthew 5:44 CJB

WORD FOCUS

Qinah: 'Jealousy', meaning to insist on exclusive devotion, tolerate no rivalry, or to have great passion for something.

DID YOU KNOW?

Matthew uses the Tanakh to show Yeshua is the Messiah.

MEMORY VERSE

"..A man who even looks at a woman with the purpose of lusting after her has already committed sin in his heart."

Luke 3:22 CJB

Matthew 5:27-28 Activity Sheet

Jealousy Grows

Jealousy has crept in and found a home where it does not belong. Remove the letters that spell 'jealousy' from these words to show what you should do instead.

Lovje youre

neighboaur las yoou

lonve ysourselfy

Jealousy

"For where there are jealousy and selfish ambition, there will be disharmony and every foul practice."

James 3:16 CJB

13

Parasha 36

Memory Verse

"Bring me seventy of the leaders of Isra'el, people you recognise as leaders of the people and officers of theirs."

Numbers 11:16 CJB

Did You Know?

The cloud of ADONAI was no ordinary cloud. It appeared as fire by night and cloud by day.

STORY SUMMARY

Priest System Set Up: The instructions for the menorah and purpose of the priesthood is explained, and their dedication ceremony outlined.

The Second Passover: Instructions are given on how to continue to keep the Pesach (Passover) and provision made for times when Pesach needs to be delayed.

The Cloud: The instructions are given for following the cloud. Also the directions for making and blowing of trumpets are given and followed.

Complaining: Isra'el complains about the manna and begs for meat and other foods. ADONAI isn't pleased with their attitude. He sets up seventy judges. Then He sends quail which makes them sick. Miryam (Miriam) also becomes sick for criticising Moshe (Moses).

WORD FOCUS

Anan: Cloud. ADONAI's presence was described like a 'pillar of cloud.' This would have looked more like a tornado than a regular fluffy cloud.

MAIN MESSAGE

The more the people disobeyed the more measures ADONAI took to protect them. He made provision for their sin by setting up the seventy Judges. This shows us ADONAI's incredible love for us but on a sad note, it shows us how our sin can cause sickness and separation from ADONAI. The more the people rebelled the greater the separation became and new systems were put in place to bridge this gap.

OBEY   **TRUST**   **BE GREATFUL**

Promise

Numbers 11:17 CJB

"...I will take some of the spirit that rests on you and put it on them. Then they will carry the burden of the people along with you, so that you won't carry it yourself alone."

Beha'alotcha Numbers 8:1-12:16 Activity Sheet

Pictorial Hebrew

Draw the ancient picture word form for 'menorah'

Name	Pictograph	Meaning	Name	Pictograph	Meaning
Aleph		Ox / strength / leader	Lamed		Staff / goad / control / "toward"
Bet		House / "In"	Mem		Water / chaos
Gimmel		Foot / camel / pride	Nun		Seed / fish / activity / life
Dalet		Tent door / pathway	Samekh		Hand on staff / support / prop
Hey		Lo! Behold! "The"	Ayin		Eye / to see / experience
Vav		Nail / peg / add / "And"	Pey		Mouth / word / speak
Zayin		Plow / weapon / cut off	Tsade		Man on side / desire / need
Chet		Tent wall / fence / separation	Qof		Sun on horizon / behind
Tet		Basket / snake / surround	Resh		Head / person / first
Yod		Arm and hand / work / deed	Shin		Eat / consume / destroy
Kaf		Palm of hand / to open	Tav		Mark / sign / covenant

_____   _____   _____   _____   _____

HEY   RESH   VAV   NUN   MEM

Quail

"The people stayed up all that day, all night and all the next day gathering quails..." Numbers 11:32 CJB

Zecharya

Zechariah 2:14-4:7

Promise

Zecharya 2:15(11)*
CJB

"...Then you will know it was *ADONAI Tzavot* who sent me to you."

* Verse 11 / 13 in other translations.

Memory Verse

"Be silent all humanity, before *ADONAI*, for He has been roused from His holy dwelling."

Zecharya 2:17(13)
*CJB

Did You Know?

Zecharya had eight visions which are recorded in the bible.

STORY SUMMARY

Y'hoshua The Priest: ADONAI makes a promise to live among His people and be the G-d of many nations. Next, the anointed High Priest Y'hoshua is on trial for his upcoming great position. HaSatan accuses him for his dirty clothes. Another angel stands up for him, saying he is 'an ember rescued from the fire.' This means he has sacrificed himself and been miraculously spared from the fire. Y'hoshua is immediately restored to his high position and his dirty clothes are removed and he is given clean ones. If he continues to be upright and do what he has been asked, he is promised access to those who are there.

WORD FOCUS

Zecharya: 'Yahweh has remembered or Yahweh remembers.'

MAIN MESSAGE

This is an amazing prophecy of Yeshua (Y'hoshua). His name is clearly given. Yeshua is on trial by HaSatan for our sins. But He is pardoned because of His selfless sacrifice and found worthy to be our High Priest and King. He is given the power to cleanse His children and raise a holy people who will be great heirs in the kingdom. When we choose Yeshua we begin that cleansing journey. It is a daily process until Yeshua comes back and fully transforms us.

YESHUA IS WORTHY   **MERCY**   **UNDESERVED FAVOUR**

Zecharya 2:14-4:7 Activity Sheet

Source of Strength

Look up Zechariah 3:9 How many eyes were on the stone? Draw them.

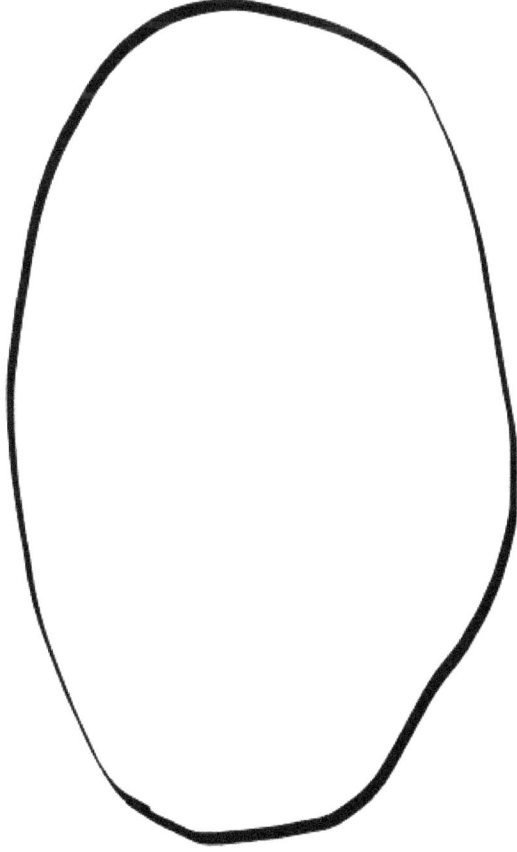

Y'hoshua Judged

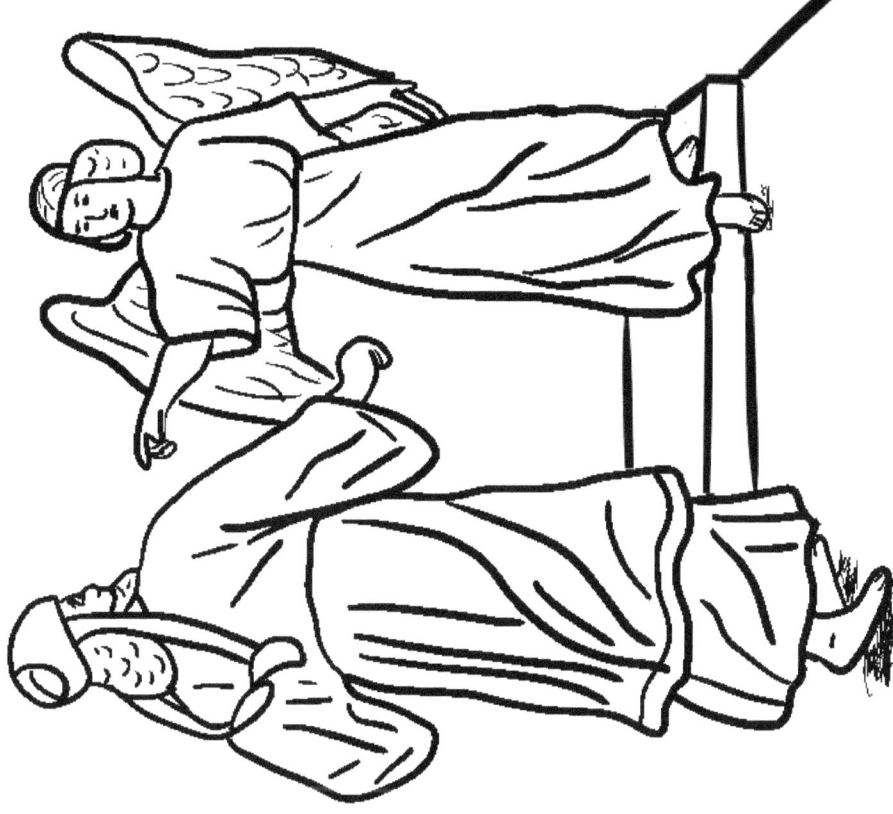

"He showed me Y'hoshua the *Cohen Hagadol* [High Priest] standing before the angel of *ADONAI* with the accuser, HaSatan at his right to accuse him." Judges 13:4 CJB

Revelation B'rit Hadashah 36
19:1-10 (Newer Testament)

STORY SUMMARY

Yeshua Begins His Reign: John sees a heavenly scene where ADONAI is being praised for His Judgements. Then there is excitement because the lamb has become King and His bride is ready.

WORD FOCUS

Nebuah: 'Prophecy.' A prophet is someone who delivers a message from ADONAI. It is usually about how people need to turn back to Him.

MEMORY VERSE

"....Worship G-d! For the testimony of Yeshua is the spirit of prophecy." Revelation 19:10 CJB

MAIN MESSAGE

The parasha spoke of the two elders that prophesied. This passage in Revelation shows us that prophecy will be a G-d given gift until the end. Those who ADONAI is pleased with at the end of time will be those who keep the commandments and have the testimony of Yeshua, which is the spirit of prophecy. Following the ways of ADONAI is still important today, and will continue to be until the end.

PROMISE

"...How blessed are those who have been invited to the wedding feast of the lamb!..." Revelation 19:9 CJB

DID YOU KNOW?

John was the last remaining apostle of his time.

Revelation 19:1-10 Activity Sheet

Revelation

Revelation means to reveal something. Write out each 3rd letter to reveal what Yeshua's message was about.

A	H	W	D	K	H	S	W	A	Z
D	T	H	U	M	G	Y	U	H	L
S	Q	R	T	C	H	L	I	A	
G	V	P	X	E	P	U	A	E	F
B	N	M	V	D	A	E	H	K	
R	F	J	Y	Y	U	S	I	C	O
Z	P	O	U	D	N	Z	I	C	O

___ ___ ___ ___

___ ___ ___ ___

The Revelation

"This is the revelation which G-d gave to Yeshua the Messiah, so that he could show His servants what must happen very soon. He communicated it by sending His angel to His servant Yochanan [John]." Revelation 1:1-2 CJB

Parasha 37

פרשת שלח לך Sh'lach L'kha (Send on your behalf) Numbers 13:1-15:41

Memory Verse

"…We ought to go up immediately and take possession of it; there is no question that we can conquer it."

Numbers 13:30 CJB

Did You Know?

Nobody that came from Egypt, apart from Joshua and Caleb, entered the Promised

STORY SUMMARY

Leaders Sent to Spy Out the Land: ADONAI tells Moshe (Moses) to gather leaders to go into Kena'an (Canaan), to see what it is like. They go for forty days and bring back grapes, figs and pomegranates. Y'hoshua (Joshua) and Kalev (Caleb) are positive the city can be overtaken, but the rest are doubtful and fearful. This makes the people doubtful and fearful also. They want to go back to Egypt. When Moshe tries to reason with them, they want to stone him. ADONAI steps in, and is about to destroy them but Moshe asks for mercy. The people are forgiven but forbidden to enter the land for another forty years. Some of them try to take the land anyway and are killed in battle. Following this story the offerings required once in the land are outlined, the penalty for breaking the Shabbat is shown, and the command to wear tzitzit (tassels) is given.

WORD FOCUS

Kena'an: From the root word *Kena*, meaning "to be brought down by a heavy load". It also can mean subdue or humble. Kena'an, in its very name was shown its destiny.

MAIN MESSAGE

Isra'el let fear guide them. They were scared and doubted they could win against the giants, even with the power of ADONAI on their side. When they let themselves believe they couldn't do it, they let fear control them and it nearly led to them stoning Moshe. Do you ever have doubting thoughts such as, *'You're not good at this'* or *'you can't do that?'* God wants to replace those thoughts with His good thoughts, such as, *'I can do it'* and *'I'm worth something'*.

TRUST   OBEY   BELIEVE

Promise

Numbers 14:24 CJB

"But My servant Kalev, because he had a different spirit with him and has fully followed Me – him I will bring into the land he entered, and it will belong to his descendants."

Sh'lach L'kha Numbers 13:1-15:41 Activity Sheet

Eye Spy

Circle the things you can find in the picture.
I spy with my little eye:

a bee, flower, rose, hat, banana, snowman, tennis ball, old mans face, rugby ball, young face, bird, wine glass, pot, sunrise, flag, and book

Delegation

"*ADONAI* said to Moshe, 'Send men on your behalf to spy out the land of Kena'an, which I am giving to the people of Isra'el.'"

Numbers 13:2 CJB

Y'hoshua

Joshua 2:1-24

Promise

Joshua 3:7 CJB

"*ADONAI* said to Y'hoshua, 'Starting today, I will make you great in full view of all Isra'el: so that they will know that just as I was with Moshe, so I will be with you.'"

STORY SUMMARY

Two Spies Sent: Two spies were sent to Yericho (Jericho) to spy out the land and report back. A woman called Rachav (Rahab) had them in her house. She told them the city was in fear of them coming, and asked them to have mercy on her family. They promised to spare her household if she hung a scarlet cloth in her window and did not betray them. She helped them escape, then kept her word. Isra'el kept their word to her too.

WORD FOCUS

Rachav: 'Wide' or 'broad'. Through her the promise land had been opened up to Isra'el.

MAIN MESSAGE

Continuing the parasha story, this shows that the Canaanites did not think of the Isra'elites as grasshoppers at all. They were fearful of them because they knew ADONAI was with them. If only Isra'el had trusted the first time. It was because of the faithfulness of Y'hoshua and Kalev that Isra'el was now able to be blessed. Rachav and her family were all spared because of her faith and willingness to help them by risking her own life. When we are faithful, others around us are blessed too.

TRUST   FAITHFULNESS   BOLDNESS

Haftara 37 (Prophets)

Memory Verse

"...I know that *ADONAI* has given you the land. Fear of you has fallen on us; everyone in the land is terrified at the thought of you."

Joshua 2:19 CJB

Did You Know?

Rachav became the mother of prophets.

Hoshea 2:1-22 Activity Sheet

Rahab

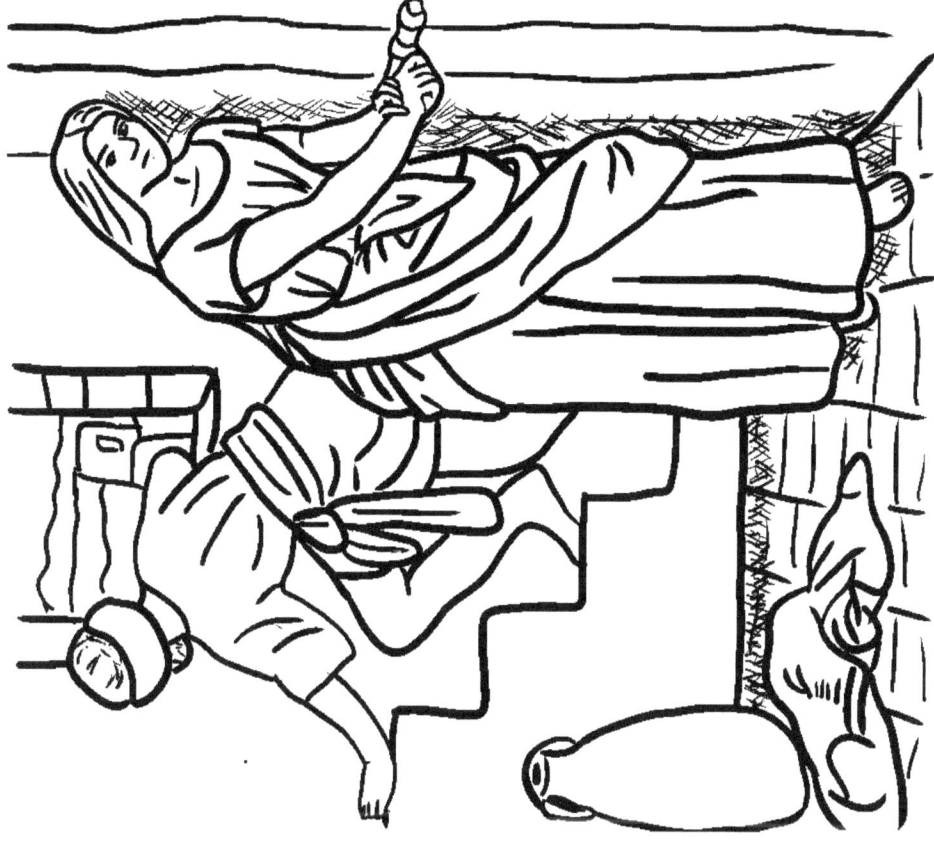

"...She had brought them up to the roof and hidden them under some stalks of flax she had spread out there." Joshua 2:6 CJB

Point of View

Isra'el spent forty years in the desert because they let their fear of the Canaanites lead them to mistrust ADONAI. They believed they were grasshoppers to the Canaanites.

Put these grasshoppers in order and write the word in the spaces provided to shows how the Canaanites really felt about the Isra'elites.

R L F A U E F

Hebrews 4:1-11

B'rit Hadashah 37
(Newer Testament)

STORY SUMMARY

Entering the Rest: Paul tells how the 'rest' of ADONAI has not completely been realised yet. This rest is based on trust. He also reaffirms the Shabbat as a time to think on this rest.

WORD FOCUS

Menuchah: 'Resting place', 'rest'. This is a rest of love freely given; of truth and sincerity; in peace and tranquillity and related to holiness. It exists that we might glorify His name.

MEMORY VERSE

"For there remains a *Shabbat*-keeping for God's people." Hebrews 4:9 CJB

MAIN MESSAGE

The promised land as received by Y'hoshua and Kalev was not the final destination in ADONAI's plan for His people. The true 'rest' has not yet come. By remembering the Shabbat and keeping it holy, we are keeping that hope alive in our hearts of the eternal promised land. Then, If we fully trust Him, we will receive full rest.

PROMISE

"Therefore, let us confidently approach the throne from which G-d gives grace, so that we may receive mercy and find grace in our time of need."
Hebrews 4:16 CJB

DID YOU KNOW?

The Shabbat is at the centre of the covenant written in stone.

Hebrews 4:1-11 Activity Sheet

Sabbath Rest

This commandment needs some rests between words to make sense.
Draw a line to separate the words to show where the rests should be.

Rememberthesabbathdaytokeep

itholy.Sixdaysshallyoulabourand

doallyourworkbuttheseventhday

isthesabbathofADONAIyourG-d.

Rest

"...Come with me by yourselves to a place where we can be alone, and you can get some rest." Mark 6:31 CJB

פרשת קורח Korakh

Numbers 16:1-18:32

Parasha 38

Memory Verse

"...The one ADONAI chooses will be the one who is holy!"

Numbers 16:7
CJB

STORY SUMMARY

Rebellion Against Moshe and Aharon: Three men start a rebellion against Moshe (Moses) and Aharon (Aaron). ADONAI is not pleased with this. Those who start the rebellion, and those who join them are destroyed. ADONAI then affirms Moshe and Aharon as His chosen leaders by causing Aharon's staff to blossom and grow almonds over night. This staff was set up in the Tabernacle to be a reminder that ADONAI had chosen him. As a result of this rebellion, the priesthood system is set up to protect the people from dying by making bad judgements.

WORD FOCUS

Qum (sounds like koom): Meaning 'to arise', or 'stand up'. This is also sometimes translated as rebel. There are good and bad things people stand up for. What things would you stand up for?

MAIN MESSAGE

A spirit of pride and self-importance led these leaders to question ADONAI's choice of leader. The people stood back and let this happen. ADONAI was not pleased with any of them. It was only when the people separated themselves from the rebels that they were spared. ADONAI does not want His people to sit back and allow evil things to happen. Have you ever watched a bully pick on someone and said nothing because you have been scared to speak out? If everyone stood together, the bully would lose his/her power.

TRUST   OBEY   BELIEVE

Promise

Numbers 18:8 CJB

"ADONAI said to Aharon, I myself have put you in charge of the contributions given to me."

Did You Know?

Korakh was a well known, respected and confident leader among the people. The people listened when he spoke.

Korakh Numbers 16:1-18:32 Activity Sheet

Rebellion

Group the same people pictures together to reveal the names of the three men that stood up against Moshe.

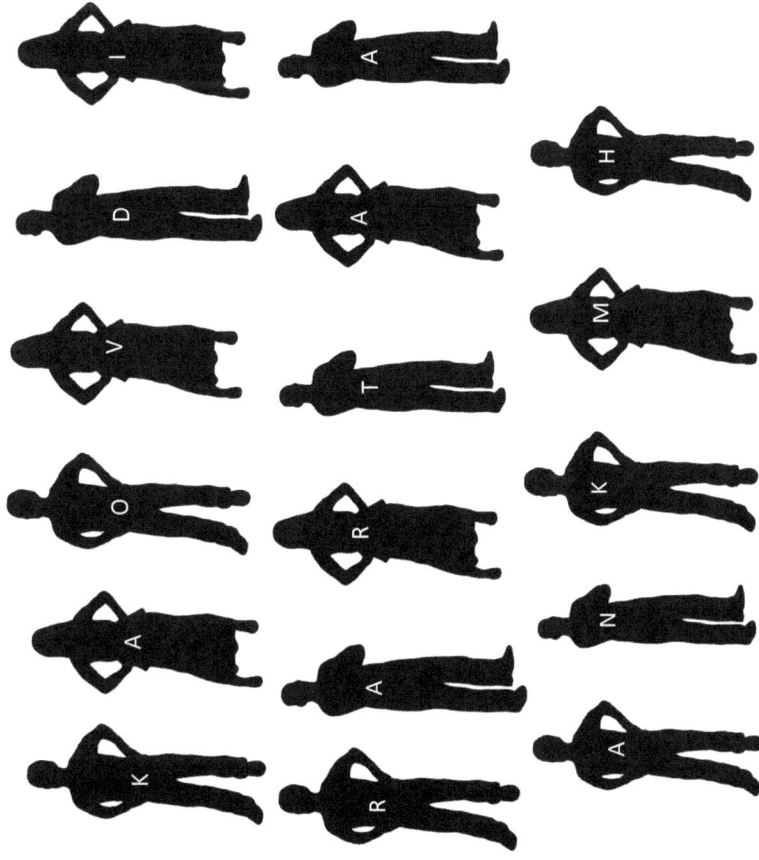

_ _ _ _ _ _ , _ _ _ _ _ _ and _ _ _ _ _

Aharon's Budding Rod

"The next day Moshe went into the tent of testimony, and there he saw that Aharon's staff for the house of Levi had budded— it had sprouted not only buds but flowers and ripe almonds as well."

Numbers 17:23(8)* CJB

* verse 8 in other translations.

Sh'muel

1 Samuel 11:14-12:22

Promise

1 Samuel 12:14 CJB

"—If both you and the king ruling you remain followers of *ADONAI* your G-d then things will go well for you."

STORY SUMMARY

A King Given: ADONAI hears the request of the people to have a king like other nations. However, Sh'muel (Samuel) is speaking against this decision. To him, this is a rejection of ADONAI as king, and a rejection of himself as a suitable representative of ADONAI. Nevertheless, ADONAI allows their choice and appoints Shaul (Saul) as king, but a warning is given. The people will only enjoy peace and blessings as long as they, and the king, follow ADONAI.

WORD FOCUS

Gilgal: Meaning 'a circle of stones'. This comes from the word **Galgal:** Meaning 'to roll away or reveal'! This was the place name where Sh'muel took the people to anoint Saul. This is also the place name where Y'hoshua (Joshua) reconfirmed the covenant of circumcision. There were a few places with this name. One meaning of 'roll away' is to commit oneself to ADONAI (Psalm 37:5).

MAIN MESSAGE

This story again shows a kind of rebellion against leadership. It also shows that ADONAI is fair and just. He is not a dictator. We can come to ADONAI with confidence that He will hear us. Our desire should be that we will make decisions that are in line with His will, not our own, because all choices have consequences. Even so, the good news is that He has planned for our mistakes too and has a 'safety net' to catch us when we fall.

RELATIONSHIP   GOOD CHOICES   FORGIVENESS

Haftara 38 (Prophets)

Memory Verse

"...For the sake of His great reputation, *ADONAI* will not abandon His people."

1 Samuel 12:22 CJB

Did You Know?

Abimelech was actually the first king of Isra'el before Saul. However, he was not chosen by ADONAI.

Judges 9:56, 22-23

Shaul Becomes King

"Come let us go to Gilgal and inaugurate the kingship there." 1 Samuel 11:14 CJB

Point of View

Use the clues in this crown to answer the question.

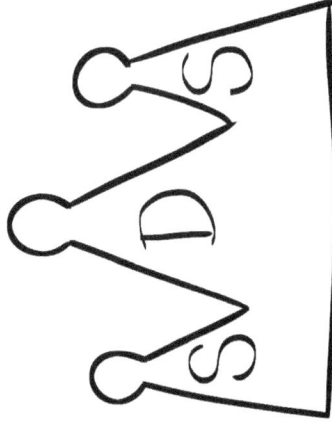

What were the names of the three appointed kings of Isra'el before it split into two kingdoms?

1. _____

2. _____

3. _____

Matthew
12:9-23

B'rit Hadashah 38
(Newer Testament)

STORY SUMMARY

Yeshua is the Appointed Servant: After Yeshua healed on Shabbat, the leaders want to get rid of Him. Yeshayahu (Isaiah) 42:1-4 is then quoted to show Yeshua is the chosen one of ADONAI. The leaders don't know how to explain His power and say it is from Baalzibbul.

WORD FOCUS

N'atsah: 'Blasphemy.' This means to either claim to be G-d or claim to be able to forgive sin. Blasphemy against the spirit means to be stubborn or hard hearted and never repent.

MEMORY VERSE

"Because of this I tell you that people will be forgiven any sin and blasphemy, but blaspheming the Ruach HaKodesh will not be forgiven." Matthew 12:32 CJB

MAIN MESSAGE

Matthew 12:31-32 tells us that blasphemy against the Spirit will not be forgiven. Maybe Korakh did this. When the leaders said Yeshua used power from HaSatan to heal, they blasphemed against the spirit. We need to be careful not to call things we do not understand a working of HaSatan. Likewise, we should not accept everything as being from ADONAI. If you are confused about something like this, pray and ask ADONAI to show you whose power is behind the action and what He wants to teach you. Also, test it against the Torah.

PROMISE

"Here is my servant, whom I have chosen, my beloved, with whom I am well pleased; I will put my Spirit on Him."
Matthew 12:18 CJB

DID YOU KNOW?

There are many verses in Tanakh that show Yeshua is the Messiah

Matthew 12:9-23 Activity Sheet

Yeshua Heals

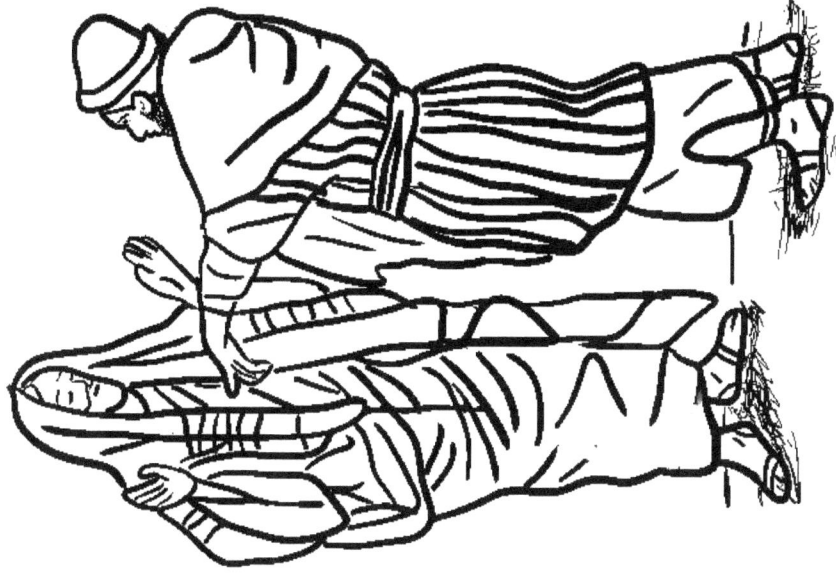

"Going from that place he went into their synagogue. A man there had a shrivelled hand ." Matthew 12:9 CJB

Healing

Yeshua heals our brokenness. Put this broken person back together again by drawing a line to connect all the pieces together again.

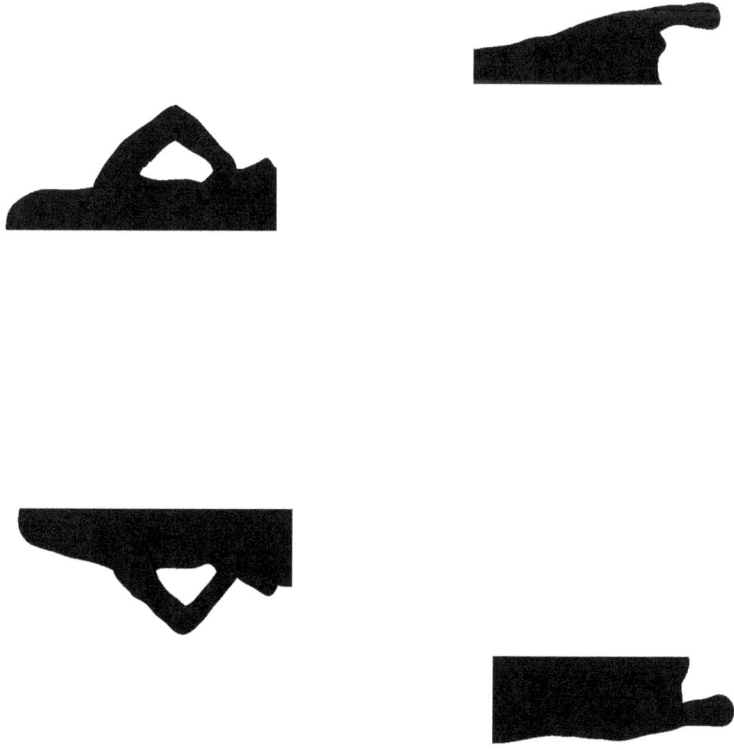

פרשת חקת Chukat (Regulation) Numbers 19:1-22:1

Parasha 39

Memory Verse

"...Because you did not trust in Me, so as to cause Me to be regarded as holy by the people of Isra'el, you will not bring this community into the land I have given them."

Numbers 20:12 CJB

Did You Know?

Yeshua fulfilled the Red Heifer sacrifice.

STORY SUMMARY

Red Heifer: The laws of the Red Heifer are set and described. After this, the death of Miriam is recorded.

Rebellion Happens: Moshe (Moses) and Aharon (Aaron) again face complaints about living conditions. ADONAI tells Moshe to speak to the rock and draw water for the people. Moshe is gruff with people, calling them rebels. Then he strikes the rock twice with his staff. Water gushes out. ADONAI then declares Moshe and Aharon will not be the ones to lead the people to the promised land. Next, Isra'el wins a battle against the Amonites. After this, Aharon dies and his son Elazar takes his role. Again, the people complain about their conditions. This time, they are sent snakes, which cause havoc. Moshe is told to make a copper snake on a pole so the people can look at it and be healed.

Isra'el Succeeds in Battle: Isra'el continues their journey, and again face enemy attack. ADONAI blesses them and allows them to take the land of Sichon and Og.

WORD FOCUS

Nehushtan: 'Piece of Brass.' This was the name given to the copper snake on the stick that Moshe made. Over time, Isra'el began to worship it, so King Hezekiah destroyed it. He called it this name to infer it had no power, but was only a 'piece of brass.'

MAIN MESSAGE

This weeks message is full of examples of how ADONAI set up measures to save His people. Yet, time after time, they did not put their trust in Him and were weakened by fear. Although ADONAI appointed Moshe and Aharon as leaders, He needed them to fully trust Him if they were ever to be successful leaders. Most of us struggle with fear. When we let fear rule, we want to do things our own way. His message is still the same today. Unless we fully trust Him, we will never be able to be used fully in His plans. Let's practice fully trusting Him so we can rise to our fullest potential.

TRUST   OBEY   BELIEVE

Promise

Numbers 21:8 CJB

" ...Make a poisonous snake and put it on a pole. When anyone who has been bitten sees it, he will live."

Chukat Numbers 19:1-22:1 Activity Sheet

Moshe Strikes the Rock

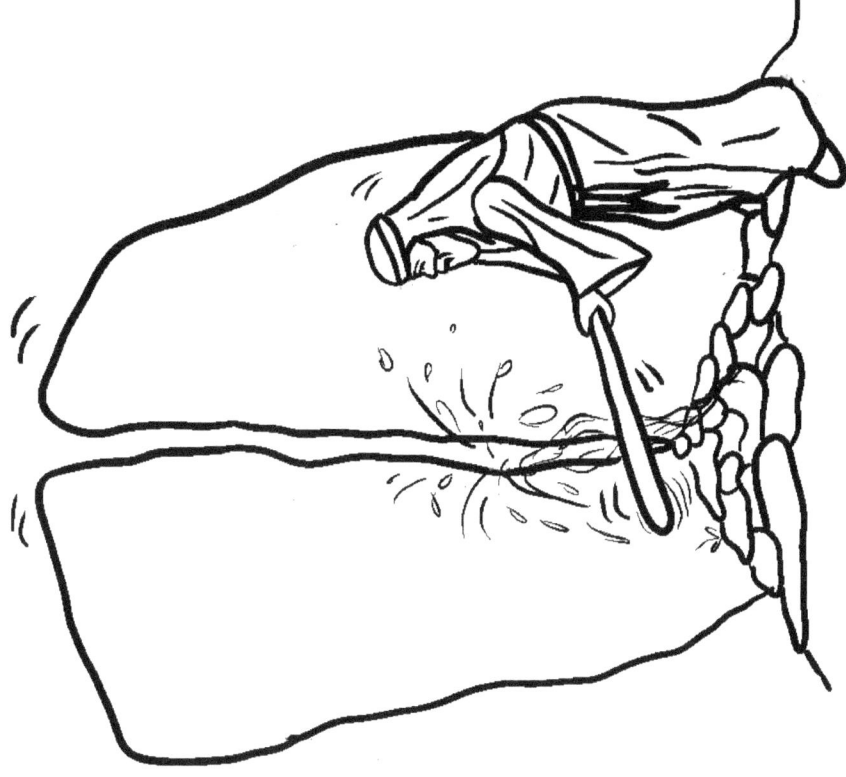

"Then Moshe raised his hand and hit the rock twice with his staff. Water flowed out in abundance, and the community and their livestock drank." Numbers 20:11 CJB

Exodus Journey

Part of the travel route is mentioned in our parasha. Draw the travel path and match the names to the numbers, starting in Kadesh in the Tzin Desert. Use the bible references to help

7. Num 21:33

6. Num 21:19

5. Num 21:13

4. Num 21:12

8.

Num 22:1

1.

Num 20:22

3.

Num 21:10

Tzin (zin) Desert

Kadesh

2.

Num 21:4

Place Names

Yericho/Jericho

Ovot/Oboth

Mt. Hor

Bashan

Zered/Zared

Suf Sea/Red Sea

Arnon

Bamot Bamoth

Shof'tim

Judges 11:1-33

Promise
Judges 11:27 CJB

"...May *ADONAI* the Judge be judge today between the people of Isra'el and the people of Amon."

STORY SUMMARY
New Battle Leader Chosen: Yiftach (Jepthah) was an outcast because his mother had a bad reputation. He left home and set up his own band of men. Because of this, he was recognised as a man who was skilled in battle. When Isra'el faced attack from the Amonites, they asked him to come back and lead them in battle. He accepted and ADONAI gave them the battle and the land.

WORD FOCUS
Yiftach: 'Opens.' Like Rachav (Rahab), Yiftach opened a way of victory for Isra'el, although he was considered an outcast.

MAIN MESSAGE
This story relates to the parasha because Amon was one of the cities which Isra'el conquered. Yiftach defended the Isra'elites right to be there, because Amon had first attacked them. Because of Yiftach's faith and trust, ADONAI allowed Amon to be defeated. Sometimes bad habits from the past come back to us. If we remember that ADONAI gave us the victory, those bad habits have no claim on us, and we can stand strong. Also, this story shows that ADONAI can use anyone. Even you.

TRUST   **HUMILITY**   **BOLDNESS**

Haftara 39 (Prophets)

Memory Verse
"So now that *ADONAI* the G-d of Isra'el has expelled the Emori before His people Isra'el, do you think that you will expel us?"

Judges 11:23 CJB

Did You Know?
Not all of the children of Isra'el settled in the Promise Land. Some stayed in lands they conquered along the way.

Judges 11:1-33 Activity Sheet

Point of View

Yiftach was in a downward spiral before he was called to help Isra'el. Circle and write down every third letter in the spiral to identify the key to Yiftach's success and favour. The first two are circled for you.

Yiftach

" ...Yiftach answered them, "If you bring me back home to fight the army of Amon, and *ADONAI* defeats them for me, I will be your head.'" Judges 11:9 CJB

John

3:9-21

B'rit Hadashah 39
(Newer Testament)

STORY SUMMARY

Yeshua and The Copper Snake: Yeshua links Himself to the copper snake by saying that He too must be lifted up like that snake if people want to live. Just as this snake was for healing, so He is for healing, and those who trust will live forever in the light.

WORD FOCUS

Chayei Olam: 'Eternal life.' Eternal life is a gift and it is found only in Yeshua who is described as being 'the life'.
(1 John 5:10-13 CJB)

MEMORY VERSE

"For G-d so loved the world that He gave His only and unique Son, so that everyone who trusts in Him may have eternal life, instead of being utterly destroyed."

John 3:16 CJB

MAIN MESSAGE

The red heifer, Y'hoshua as the new leader, and the copper snake all point to Yeshua. Through Yeshua, what once was impossible is now possible. If we hold Him up, and keep our eyes on Him, He has promised to save us.

PROMISE

"Just as Moshe lifted up the serpent in the desert, so must the Son of Man be lifted up; so that everyone who trusts in Him may have eternal life."

John 3:14-15 CJB

DID YOU KNOW?

Just as the snake on the pole became an idol then, these days images of Yeshua on the cross have become and idol to some people today.

John 3:9-21 Activity Sheet

Serpent on the Rod

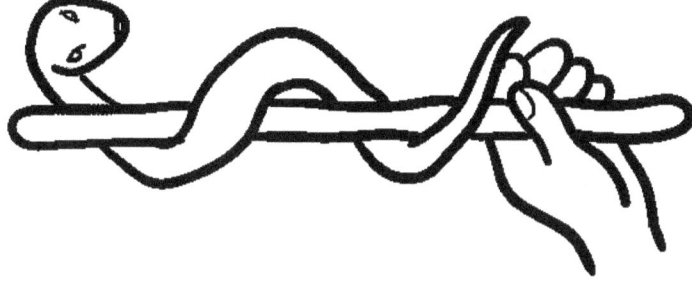

"Just as Moshe lifted up the serpent in the desert, so must the Son of Man be lifted up; so that everyone who trusts in Him may have eternal life." John 3:14-15 CJB

Eternal life

Can you remember John 3:16 without reading it?

For _____

_____

_____

_____

_____

_____

_____

_____

בלק Balak

Numbers 22:2–25:9

Parasha 40

Memory Verse

"G-d is not a human who lies or a mortal who changes His mind. When He says something, He will do it; when He makes a promise He will fulfil it."

Numbers 20:12 CJB

Did You Know?

The Moabites were related to Isra'el through Abraham's nephew, Lot.

Promise

Numbers 24:7 CJB

"Water will flow from their branches, their seed will have water aplenty. Their king will be higher than Agag and his kingdom lifted high."

STORY SUMMARY

Balak Seeks the Help of Bil'am: When Balak, the king of Mo'av (Moab) sees the Isra'elites come and set up camp next to his city, he is scared of them. He sends for Bil'am (Balaam) to curse Isra'el. Bil'am is a sorcerer who is well known for cursing and blessing. Bil'am is familiar with Isra'el's God. ADONAI comes to Bil'am and tells him not to curse Isra'el, because they are blessed by him. Bil'am refuses to go with the men, but Balak doesn't take no for an answer. He sends more messengers and offers more money. This time, when Bil'am asks, ADONAI allows him to go, but only to speak as ADONAI directs. Bil'am goes, but ADONAI isn't happy about it, and sends an angel to block his way. Bil'am's donkey sees the angel but Bil'am doesn't. Three times he beats his donkey until the angel allows the donkey to speak and ask why she is being beaten. Bil'am is shown the angel and repents. However, ADONAI tells him to continue the trip and again speak only as directed. Balak takes Bil'am to different locations where they can see the camp of Isra'el and asks Bi'am to curse them, but he blesses them instead. Despite this, the reading ends with Isra'el's rebellion by worshiping Baal, and as a result suffering another plague.

WORD FOCUS

Balak: From the word 'balaq 'meaning 'to waste' or 'lay waste'. Although Balak intended to live up to his name and 'lay waste' the people of Isra'el, ADONAI had other plans.

MAIN MESSAGE

It may seem confusing why ADONAI was angry with Bil'am from reading this story. Although ADONAI allowed Bil'am to go, ADONAI had clearly said before that He was not to go and why. Perhaps ADONAI could see Bil'am actually wanted to go and was tempted by the money and prestige. Whatever the reason, ADONAI used this heart condition to bring about even further blessings to His people, and to show Bil'am up. One thing we can learn from this story is that although ADONAI sometimes appears to allow wickedness, there is always either a consequence or a greater outcome for the glory of ADONAI. One of the most famous messianic prophecies comes out of Bil'am blessing.

TRUST   OBEY   RESPECT

Balak Numbers 22:2-25:9 Activity Sheet

Speaking Donkey

Look up Numbers 22:28 to find the words the donkey spoke to Bil'am.

Write the words in the speech Bubble.

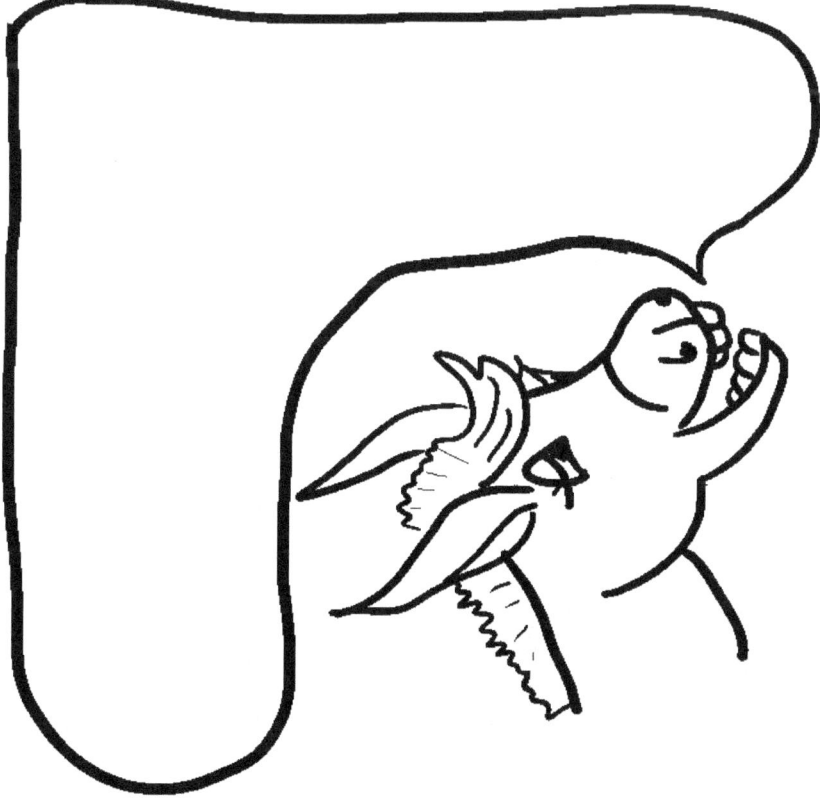

Bil'am

"Again the donkey saw the angel of ADONAI and lay down under Bil'am, which made him so angry that he hit the donkey with a stick." Numbers 22:27CJB

Mikhah

Micah 5:6(7)*-6:8

Promise

Micah 5:6(7)* CJB

"Then the remnant of Ya'akov (Jacob), surrounded by many peoples, will be like dew from *ADONAI*, like showers on the grass, which doesn't wait for a man or expect anything from mortals."

Haftara 40 (Prophets)

Memory Verse

"Human being, you have already been told what is good, what *ADONAI* demands of you– no more than to act justly, love grace and walk in purity with your G-d."

Micah 6:8 CJB

Did You Know?

Mikhah prophesied during the times of Kings Jotham, Ahaz and Hezekiah.

STORY SUMMARY

Isra'els Future Status: ADONAI, speaking through Micah, describes a time where Isra'el will be as a lion among the forest animals and sheep. They will no longer be subject to other nations. Then the scene changes to a court setting where ADONAI has His people on trial, and reminds them of all He has done for them. Then, instead of condemning them, He encourages them.

WORD FOCUS

Chesed: 'Grace', as translated in the CJB version of Micah 6:8, but is actually said to be the main characteristic of ADONAI. It is also translated as 'kindness', 'love', 'mercy' and most fittingly 'loyal love' or 'covenant loyalty'.

MAIN MESSAGE

Have you ever heard anyone say, "I can talk about my family the way I want but if anyone else says anything against them watch out?" The same kind of thing is happening in this story. The nations were eagerly waiting for ADONAI to condemn His children. Instead He blesses and encourages them; promising restoration and elevated status among the nations. ADONAI's love for you never fails. When you are His, and others stand against you, He will defend you.

LOYALTY   MERCY   GRACE

* Verse 7 in other translations.

Mikhah 5:6-6:8 Activity Sheet

Bil'am Blesses Isra'el

"My people, just remember what Balak the king of Mo'av had planned, what Bil'am the son of B'or answered him, and what happened between Sheetim and Gilgal-so that you understand the saving deeds of *ADONAI.*" Micah 6:5 CJB

Speak Blessings

ADONAI wants us to use our words to bless, not curse, each other. Put an **X** through the phrases that would be a curse to someone and a tick next to the words of blessing

I hate you

You are a good friend

I'm not your friend

You are a blessing

God loves you

You're a cry baby

You are ugly

I like you

Nobody likes you

You are good for nothing

You are precious

Revelation   B'rit Hadashah 40
22:16   (Newer Testament)

STORY SUMMARY

Yeshua Identifies Himself: Yeshua comes to John in vision and identifies Himself as the Root and Offspring of David, the bright Morning Star.

WORD FOCUS

Magen David: 'Star of David.' Because the Messiah is described in Numbers as the 'Morning Star', this has been a symbol of messianic hope for the Jewish people throughout many generations.

MEMORY VERSE

"I Yeshua, have sent My angel to give you this testimony for the messianic communities. I am the Root and Offspring of David, the bright Morning Star." Revelation 22:16 CJB

MAIN MESSAGE

In this verse, Yeshua is showing that He is the one referred to in this earlier prophecy in Numbers. In verse 20 He leaves us with the promise that He is coming soon.

PROMISE

"I see him but not now; I behold him, but not soon-a star will step forth from Ya'akov (Jacob) a scepter will arise from Isra'el..."   Number 24:17 CJB

DID YOU KNOW?

Yeshua is a descendant of David through His mother, and His earthly father.

Revelation 22:16 Activity Sheet

Dot to Dot

Complete the dot to dot to form the picture.

13 ● 1

● 2   ● 3

● 4

● 5

● 12   ● 6

● 7

● 10   ● 8

● 11   ● 9

Angel of Yeshua

"I Yeshua, have sent My angel to give you this testimony for the messianic communities. I am the Root and Offspring of David, the bright Morning Star." Revelation 22:16 CJB

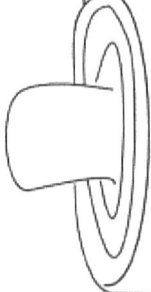

פִּינְחָס Pinchas (Phinehas) Numbers 25:10-30:1(29:40)*

Parasha 41

Memory Verse

"This is because he was zealous on behalf of his G-d and made atonement for the people of Isra'el."

Numbers 25:12 CJB

Did You Know?

It was Bil'am's advice to Balak which caused Isra'el to sin.

STORY SUMMARY

Pinchas Blessed: ADONAI rewards Pinchas for being zealous, and stopping the spread of idolatry in the camp. Then Isra'el goes to war with Midian and takes another census of the men over 20. There were over six hundred thousand men.

Tzelafchad's Daughters Inherit: It was decided, when there were no sons in a family, females were allowed to inherit land.

Y'hoshua Chosen: Y'hoshua (Joshua) is chosen to be the leader of Isra'el in place of Moshe (Moses).

Sacrifices Described: Requirements for various sacrifices are given.

WORD FOCUS

Shalom: 'Peace' or 'to be whole or sound – Complete', To be complete is to be healthy in soul and spirit.

MAIN MESSAGE

This portion has a number of themes in it; being zealous, showing justice, true leadership and perfection in numbers. Firstly, because Pinchas is passionate about ADONAI, he stands up against the spread of evil. However, he is not the leader ADONAI appoints, this leader will be more shepherd like. Next, the daughters find justice, and an example of treating people justly is set. Finally, when the animal sacrifices are studied, many have seen number patterns showing. ADONAI is trying to give an important message through these sacrifices. The more they are studied, the more comparisons are made. The Bible is full of wonders to discover, often hidden in details we may consider boring and not necessary for our lives.

COMPASSION   JUSTICE   PASSION

Promise

Numbers 25:11 CJB

"I am giving him My covenant of shalom, making a covenant with him and his descendants after him that the office of *cohen* will be theirs forever."

* Verse 29:40 in other translations

44

Pinchas Numbers 25:10-30:1 Activity Sheet

Sacrifices

Solve the sums to answer how many cow sacrifices were required for each day of Sukkot.

Day 1 $20-7=$ _____

Day 2 $6 \times 2=$ _____

Day 3 $5+6$ _____

Day 4 $20 \div 2=$ _____

Day 5 $16-7=$ _____

Day 6 $4+4=$ _____

Day 7 $14 \div 2=$ _____

Y'hoshua Chosen

"ADONAI said to Moshe, "Take Y'hoshua the son of Nun, a spiritual man, and lay your hand on him. Put him in front of El'azar the *cohen* and the whole community, and commission him in their sight..."

Numbers 27:18-19 CJB

M'lakim Alef

1 Kings 18:46-19:21

Haftara 41 (Prophets)

Memory Verse

"...Suddenly an angel touched him and said to him 'Get up and eat!'"

1 Kings 19:5 CJB

Did You Know?

ADONAI made a comparison with Moshe when He took Eliyahu to the same mountain. Even when ADONAI showed up in fire and earthquake, the people still made the calf.

Promise

1 Kings 19:11-12 CJB

"He said, 'Go outside, and stand on the mountain before ADONAI'; and right then and there, ADONAI went past. A mighty blast of wind tore the mountains apart and broke the rocks in pieces before ADONAI, but ADONAI was not in the wind. After the wind came an earthquake, but ADONAI was not in the earthquake. After the earthquake, fire broke out; but ADONAI was not in the fire. And after the fire came a quiet, subdued voice."

STORY SUMMARY

Eliyahu (Elijah) Runs for His Life: Elijah had just shown up the gods of Baal by calling down fire from heaven. He hoped the people would change their ways, but now his life is being threatened by queen Izevel (Jezebel). He runs into the wilderness and is so depressed he wants to die. ADONAI sends and angel to feed him, then leads him to Mt. Horev where ADONAI shows him great displays. However, ADONAI tells Eliyahu that He is not in these displays but in the still small voice. When Eliyahu returns home, Elisha is appointed to take over the role of prophet.

WORD FOCUS

Qinah: 'Ador', 'zeal', 'jealousy.' Jealousy, as written in some verses, is not the same as we view it today. It is more related to 'zeal', which is an intense love for something or someone.

MAIN MESSAGE

Like Pinchas, Elijah was very zealous for ADONAI. In this story ADONAI tries to teach Elijah that the changing of people's hearts is not going to come through miracles and great displays but through the still small voice that talks to each one individually. This can take time. We need to make sure that we are not always looking for great displays of ADONAI, but taking time to stop and listen to the still small voice.

QUIETNESS   LISTENING   RELATIONSHIP

An Angel Feeds Eliyahu

"The angel came again, a second time, touched him and said, 'Get up and eat, or the journey will be too much for you.'"

1 Kings 19:7 CJB

The Way to ADONAI

ADONAI said it was not in the big displays that He is found. Match up the broken hearts and number them in order to complete the sentence and find out where ADONAI is found.

still

small

the

in

voice

ADONAI is

Matthew
9:36

B'rit Hadashah 41
(Newer Testament)

STORY SUMMARY

Yeshua Has Compassion: Yeshua sees the desperate needs of the people, and His heart aches, because they do not have a strong leader to follow.

WORD FOCUS

Ro'eh, Ro'i: 'Shepherd.' Psalms 23 says ADONAI is our shepherd. It is His desire to be our leader. He wants to feed us and tend to our needs.

MEMORY VERSE

"When He saw the crowds, He had compassion on them because they were harried and helpless, like sheep without a shepherd." Matthew 9:36 CJB

MAIN MESSAGE

The desire for a strong leader of Isra'el is recorded in Numbers 27:15-17, just before Y'hoshua is appointed. Y'hoshua was a symbol of the messiah. Yeshua is the only one who has matched the description fully.

PROMISE

"Moshe said to ADONAI, 'Let ADONAI, G-d of the spirits of all human beings, appoint a man to be over the community, to go out and come in ahead of them, to lead them out and bring them in, so that ADONAI's community will not be like sheep without a shepherd.'"   Number 27:15-17 CJB

DID YOU KNOW?

Yeshua and Y'hoshua share the same name.

Matthew 9:36 Activity Sheet

Shepherd

"*ADONAI* is my shepherd; I lack nothing. He has me lie down in grassy pastures, He leads me by quiet water, He restores my inner person. He guides me in right paths for the sake of His own name." Psalm 23:1-3 CJB

A Good Leader

Shepherd the sheep through this maze to find the green pasture in the middle.

משה מטות Matot (Tribes) Numbers 30:2(1)*-32:42

Parasha 42

Memory Verse

"When a man makes a vow to ADONAI or formally obligates himself by swearing an oath, he is not to break his word but is to do everything he said he would do."

Numbers 30:3(2)* CJB

Did You Know?

The tribes of Reuven (Reuben) and Gad never settled in the promised land.

STORY SUMMARY

Rules for Swearing an Oath: Moshe tells Isra'el what ADONAI said about making oaths or vows and when they must be kept or may be broken.

Isra'el Goes to War Against Midian: Because the Midianites tried to corrupt and curse Isra'el, ADONAI sends Isra'el to war against them. When they come back with captives, Moshe isn't pleased they spared the women who caused Isra'el to fall. Moshe and Elazar the priest, give Isra'el more instructions on how to be clean. Then, the animals they took from Midian are distributed among Isra'el.

Reuven and Gad Request to Stay: The tribes of Reuven and Gad see the land is good for grazing and request to stay. They make an agreement with Moshe for the men to help Isra'el fight their way to Caanan but leave their wives, children and cattle in cities and pens they will build.

WORD FOCUS

Qatsaph: 'To become angry'. We should not be quick tempered but be slow to anger.

MAIN MESSAGE

ADONAI is showing the importance of our words. We should think carefully before we speak. Moshe lost his temper and wasn't able to give Isra'el all the instructions needed on his own. When we get angry we lose our wisdom and ability to be effective. Also this portion shows us that ADONAI is the avenger of His people. When we let Him take this role instead of us, we can be free of the hatred that comes from plotting revenge. We also see that ADONAI is a reasonable G-d and is happy to talk things through with us.

CAREFUL SPEECH   JUSTICE   RELATIONSHIP

Promise

Numbers 32:20-22 CJB

"Moshe said to them, 'If you will do this — if you will arm yourselves to go before ADONAI to the war, and if every one of your soldiers will cross the Yarden before ADONAI, until he has driven out his enemies ahead of him, and if the land has been conquered before ADONAI, and only after that do you return — then you will be clear before ADONAI/ and before Isra'el, and this land here will be yours to possess before ADONAI...'"

Note: Parental discretion advised when reading biblical narrative.

* Verse in other translations

Matot Numbers 30:2-32:42 Activity Sheet

Fortified City

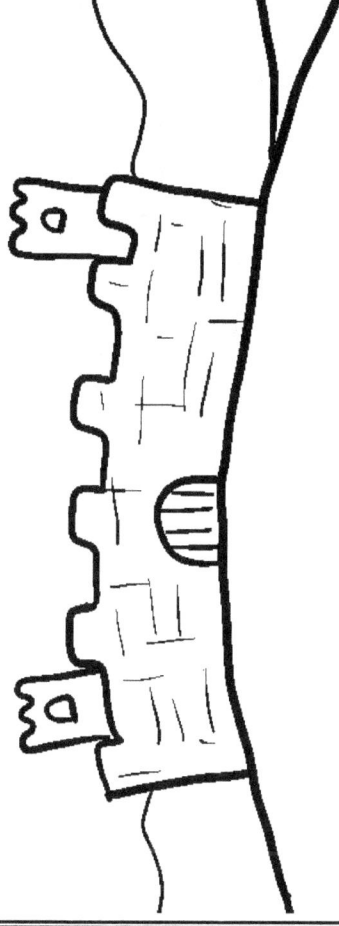

"…Here we will build enclosures for our livestock and cities for our little ones." Numbers 32:16CJB

One Fiftieth

One fiftieth of the livestock was kept for ADONAI. What is 1/50 of these flocks.

50 Sheep =

150 Donkeys =

200 Cattle =

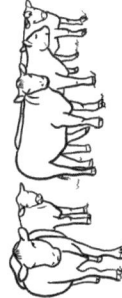

Haftara of Affliction 1.

Jeremiah 1:1-2:3

Promise

Jeremiah 1:5 CJB

"Before I formed you in the womb, I knew you; before you were born, I separated you for myself. I have appointed you to be a prophet to the nations."

STORY SUMMARY

Yirmeyahu (Jeremiah) Appointed as Prophet: Yirmeyahu tells how ADONAI chose him to be a prophet before he was born. When Yirmeyahu tries to make excuses by saying he is too young, ADONAI will not hear of it. Yirmeyahu is then sent two visions. One vision is of the almond tree branch, and the other of a burning caldron, spilling out towards the south, and coming from the north. ADONAI then explains the second vision is about a time of trouble coming. He tells Yirmeyahu to go and give this message to the people.

WORD FOCUS

Shiva Asar B'Tammuz: The fast of the '17th of Tammuz'. For three weeks, Haftara readings don't follow the parasha reading but are in line with the 'Mourning of Jerusalem'. This is a rememberance of Isra'el's past calamities. Two of these calamities led to the destruction of the first and second Temples.

MAIN MESSAGE

This story shows us that we are never to young to follow ADONAI's plan for us. If He has called us, He will give us the gifts we need to obey. We can also know that ADONAI cares for us and knows us intimately. He is keenly interesting in our growth and development. The first vision signified that just as the almond branch was quick to blossom, ADONAI would be quick to bring about the prophecy.

CHOSEN   TRUST   STRENGTH

Memory Verse

"But *ADONAI* said to me, "Don't say, 'I'm just a child.'

'For you will go to whomever I send you, and you will speak whatever I order you. Do not be afraid of them, for I am with you, says *ADONAI*, to rescue you.'"

Jeremiah 1:7-8 CJB

Did You Know?

Many rabbis say Yirmeyahu was a descendant of Y'shohua (Joshua) and Rachav (Rahab).

Haftara of Affliction 1. Jeremiah 1:1-2:3 Activity Sheet

Almond Tree Branch

"The word of ADONAI came to me, asking, 'Yirmeyahu, what do you see?' I answered, 'I see a branch from an almond tree.'"

Jeremiah 1:11 CJB

Enemies Of Isra'el

Jeremiah 2:3 tells the fate of those who 'devour' Isra'el. Decode the message to find out.

Matthew
5:33-37 (Newer Testament)

B'rit Hadashah 42

STORY SUMMARY

Yeshua Expands on Making Oaths: Yeshua challenges the people about not breaking a vow. We should not promise an oath in the first place. Instead just say 'yes' or 'no' and keep our word as best we can.

WORD FOCUS

Neder: 'Vow' This usually has an offering attached.
Shebua: 'Oath' This is a strong promise. It could be a blessing or a curse.

MEMORY VERSE

"Just let your 'yes' be a simple 'yes', and your 'no' a simple 'no'; anything more than this has its origin in evil."
Matthew 5:37 CJB

MAIN MESSAGE

In the style used by other rabbi's of the time, Yeshua challenges the people on points of the law, showing how important our words are. It is not good to make promises we may not be able to keep. Especially bringing down ADONAI's reputation by swearing on things He has made. However, we should make every effort to do the things we say we will do. This makes us trustworthy.

PROMISE

"He who guards his mouth and his tongue, guards his soul from troubles." Proverbs 21:23

DID YOU KNOW?

ADONAI spoke and the universe came into being. Words have the power to build up and tear down.

Matthew 5:33-37 Activity Sheet

Teaching on the Mount

"Seeing the crowds, Yeshua walked up the hill. After He sat down, His *talmidim* came to Him and He began to speak. This is what He taught them." Matthew 5:1-2 CJB

Power of Words

There is one things that can cut deeper than a knife. Use the first letter of each picture to uncover what it is.

Parasha 43

משה מסעי **Masei** (Stages) Numbers 33:1-36:13

Promise

Numbers 33:53 CJB

"Drive out the inhabitants of the land, and live in it, for I have given the land to you as a possession."

Memory Verse

"G-d is our refuge and strength, an ever-present help in trouble."

Psalms 46:2(1)* CJB

Did You Know?

Yeshua paid the penalty for our sin. His life was given so our lives may be spared.

STORY SUMMARY

Exodus Journey Outlined: Every location Isra'el camped at is listed here in order.

Land Allocation Explained: Each tribe was given different pieces of land. ADONAI tells them exactly where their land is to be, and who would be responsible for dividing it. The Levites did not inherit land, so ADONAI tells them where to live and have land. In the cities given to the Levites, ADONAI makes special provision for people who have accidently killed someone. They may flee to these cities and be safe. They must stay there as long as the High Priest lives. When he dies they may return. During the dividing of the land, the dispute about women inheriting land comes up again. It is decided that woman who inherit land need to marry within their own tribe. This is so the land still belongs to the tribe it was originally given to.

WORD FOCUS

Miqlat: 'Refuge' or 'Asylum'. To take refuge means to be safe and sheltered from harm. ADONAI is also personally described as our refuge.

MAIN MESSAGE

ADONAI is showing how He led the people out of Egypt to the Promised Land according to His plan and purpose. He also shows His great compassion by allowing for the cities of refuge.

ADONAI IS OUR PROTECTOR, PROVIDER AND SHEPHERD

* Verse 1 in other translations

Masei Numbers 33:1-36:13 Activity Sheet

The Exodus Route of Numbers 33

In Lesson 39 we studied the route from Kadesh to Caanan. This lesson fills in the places before Kadesh also. This map shows a possible route Isra'el may have taken, and lists all the stops. Some of the main possible locations are shown. Connect the numbers to make a trail. Some numbers are skipped.

1. Ramses
2. Sukkot
3. Etam
4. Pi Hachirot
5. Sea of suf
6. Marah
7. Elilim
8. Seen desert
9. Dofkah
10. Alush
11. Refidim
12. Sanai Desert
13. Kivrot-HaTa'avah
14. Hatzerot
15. Ritmah
16. Rimmon-Peretz

17. Livnah
18. Rissah
19. K'helah
20. Mt Shefer
21. Haradah
22. Mak'helot
23. Tachat
24. Terach
25. Mitkah
26. Ha Shmonah
27. Moserot
28. B'nei-Ya'akan
29. Hor-HaGidgad
30. Yotvatah
31. Avronah
32. Etzyon-Gever
33. Kadesh

EGYPT

Promise

Jeremiah 4:1-2
CJB

"'Isra'el, if you will return,' says ADONAI, 'yes, return to me; and if you will banish your abominations from my presence without wandering astray again; and if you will swear, *As ADONAI lives,* in truth, justice and righteousness; then the nations will bless themselves by Him, and in Him will they glory.'"

Haftara of Affliction 2

Jeremiah 2:4-28; 4:1-2

STORY SUMMARY

ADONAI Laments Over Isra'el: ADONAI, through Yirmeyahu, tells how His children have turned their back on Him. You can hear the earnest call of ADONAI as He asks them what He has done to deserve this. Even the heathens have not turned against their god's, as Isra'el has turned against ADONAI. He is pleading with them to change their ways. If they do, the whole world will be blessed.

WORD FOCUS

Maqor: the fountain, **mayim:** waters, **chay:** of living. 'The fountain of Living Water.' This is the description ADONAI gives Himself in Jeremiah 2:13. This is what people are giving up by rejecting Him.

MAIN MESSAGE

This is the second of three lessons focusing on the mistakes of ADONAI's people. Have you ever lost a friendship or felt rejection by someone you care about. Maybe you too have asked the question, "What is wrong with me?" If you have then you can understand a little about how ADONAI feels when we walk away from, or rebel against Him. We can also know ADONAI understands our pain when we feel rejected.

EMPATHY   **ACCEPTANCE**   **LOYALTY**

Haftara 43 (Prophets)

Memory Verse

"What did your ancestors find wrong with me to make them go so far away from me..."
Jeremiah 2:5
CJB

Did You Know?

Yeshua also called Himself the living water in John 4

Haftara of Affliction 2. Jeremiah 2:4-28 Activity Sheet

Fountain of life

Drinking from the right fountain brings life, and drinking from the wrong fountain makes you more thirsty. Choose the right water droplets to complete the verse. Cross out the wrong water droplets.

"But whoever _____ the _____ be

_____ again!" John 4:14 CJB

eats

thirsty

water

dirt

hungry

always

smells

drinks

never

Broken Cistern

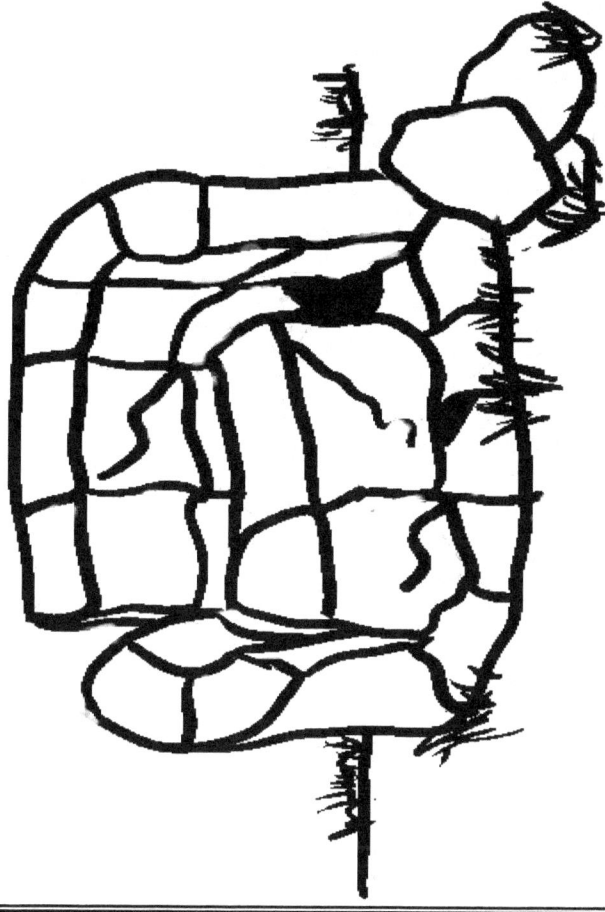

"For my people have committed two evils: they have abandoned me, the fountain of living water, and dug themselves cisterns, broken cisterns, that can hold no water!" Jeremiah 2:13 CJB

Matthew

18:15-17

B'rit Hadashah 43
(Newer Testament)

STORY SUMMARY

Dealing With Conflict: Yeshua says if you have a problem with somebody, you should go alone to the person. If the person won't listen, take one or two witnesses. Then, tell the congregation. If the person still will not listen, treat them as you would an unbeliever.

WORD FOCUS

Ed: 'A witness.' Two witnesses were required to bring a judgement in the Torah. Yeshua confirms this principle in Matthew 18.

MEMORY VERSE

"If he refuses to hear them, tell the congregation; and if he refuses to listen even to the congregation, treat him as you would a pagan or a tax-collector." Matthew 18:17 CJB

MAIN MESSAGE

On the topic of witnesses, Yeshua is consistent with the laws given in the Torah. Also, just as ADONAI showed compassion by allowing the cities of refuge, Yeshua is showing compassion with how to treat a brother or sister who is in sin. Even if they won't listen, we are are not to cut them off, but to consider them as a non-believer. Therefore, they become someone who needs to be reached again for His kingdom.

PROMISE

"Moreover, if your brother commits a sin against you, go and show him his fault — but privately, just between the two of you. If he listens to you, you have won back your brother."

Matthew 18:15 CJB

DID YOU KNOW?

Revelation also tells of two witnesses that will speak for Yeshua in the final conflict.

Matthew 18:15-17 Activity Sheet

Witnesses

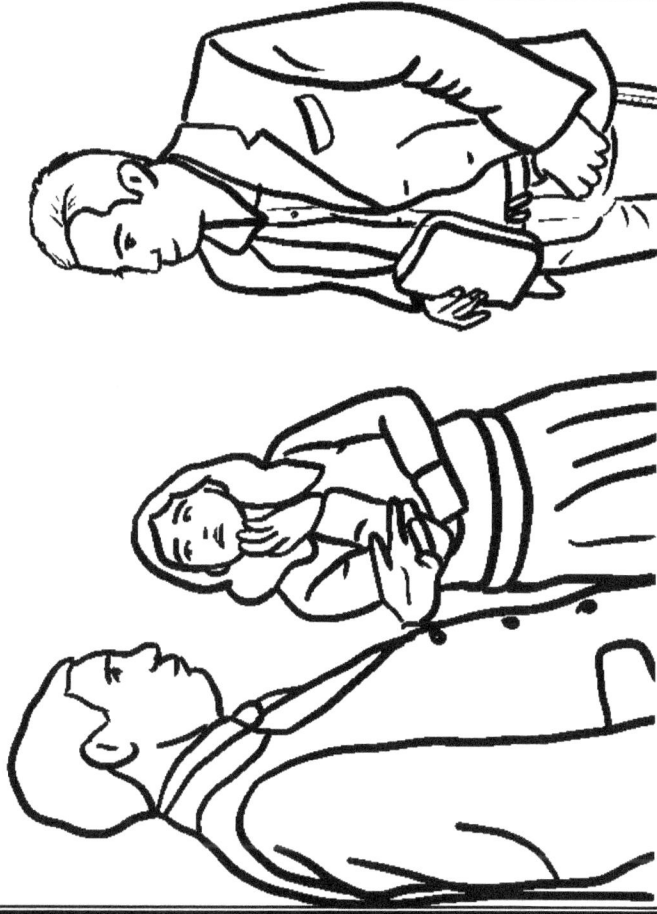

"If he doesn't listen, take one or two others with you so that every accusation can be supported by the testimony of two or three witnesses." Matthew 18:16 CJB

A Brother in Sin

Yeshua says we should talk to each other about our sins. Brainstorm and write down or draw some things that are sins. Is there something you need to be sorry for?

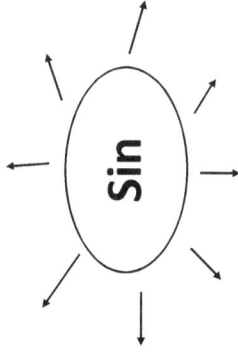

Sin

Answers

Parasha 34 For more info on the flags see:
judaism.stackexchange.com/questions/23496/
what-are-the-symbols-of-the-12-tribes

Haftara 34

Parasha 35

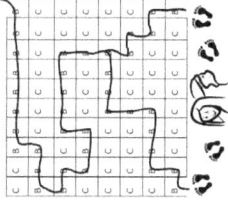

Haftara 35

```
THE SOURCE OF SH
IMSHON'S STRENG
TH WAS IN HIS HAIR.
IF HIS HAIR WAS TO B
E CUT HE WOULD LO
SE HIS STRENGTH.
```

B'rit Hadasha 35

Love your neighbour (as you love yourself)

Parasha 36

HEY   RESH   VAV   NUN   MEM

Haftara 36

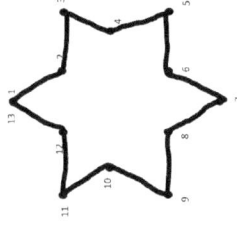

B'rit Hadashah 36

WHAT MUST HAPPEN VERY SOON

Parasha 37

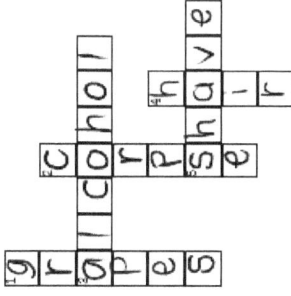

Haftara 37   FEARFUL

B'rit Hadashah 37

Remember the sabbath day to keep it holy. Six days shall you labour and do all your work but the seventh day is the sabbath of ADONAI your G-d.

Parasha 38

Korakh, Datan, and Aviram

Haftara 38

Saul, David, Shlomo (Solomon)

B'rit Hadashah 38

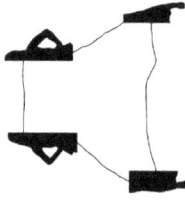

Parasha 39

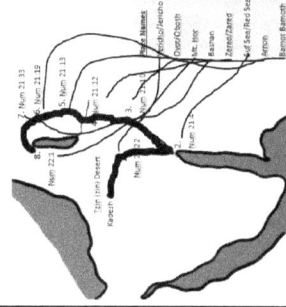

Haftara 39   Trust and Faith.

Parasha 40   What have I done to you to make you beat me these three times?"

Haftara 40

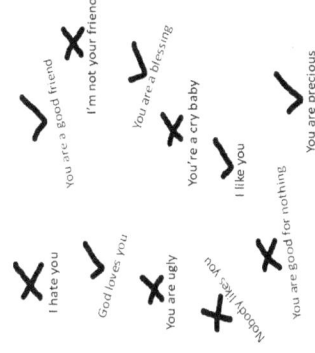

I hate you
You are a good friend
God loves you
I'm not your friend
You are ugly
You are a blessing
You're a cry baby
Nobody likes you
I like you
You are good for nothing
You are precious

B'rit Hadashah 40

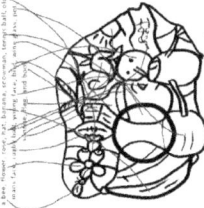

Parasha 41

13,12,11,10,9,8,7

Haftara 41

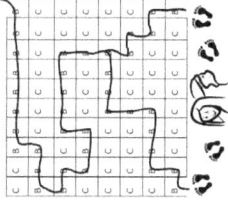

B'rit Hadashah 41

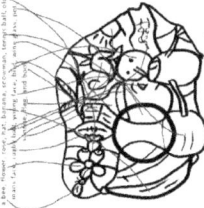

Parasha 42

1,3,4

Haftara 42

They will be guilty and evil will befall them.

B'rit Hadashah 42

The tongue

Parasha 43

Haftara 43

drinks, water, never, thirsty.

B'rit Hadasha 43

Answers will vary but may include lying, cheating stealing, etc.

drinks, water, never, thirsty.

---

shavuot

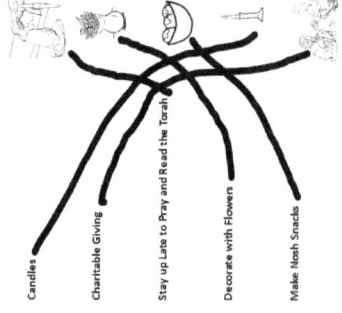

Candles
Charitable Giving
Stay up Late to Pray and Read the Torah
Decorate with Flowers
Make Noah Snacks

Shavuot

Giving of the Torah and the Ruach HaShem

WHAT IS SHAVUOT? Shavuot is the Feast of Weeks. The seven weeks that were counted after the Pesach Sabbath.

WHEN IS SHAVUOT? At the end of the 50 day count of the omer (sheaves) since Pesach.

WHAT DO WE DO ON SHAVUOT? It is a celebration time connected to first fruits. Yeshua was the first fruits of the resurrection. This bread represents His people that are also to be presented to ADONAI and accepted. It is a holy Shabbat day to pray and to bring a thanks giving offering to ADONAI.

WHAT HAS HAPPENED ON THIS DAY IN HISTORY? On this day the giving of the Torah to Moshe (Moses) at Mt. Horev is celebrated. This is the anniversary of the covenant between ADONAI and Isra'el. We also recognise on this day many years later, the promised Rauch Ha Kodesh (Holy Spirit) was given. Many believe this to be the time when the new covenant promise of Jeremiah 31:33 began to happen. When the Ruach (Spirit) came many people recognised their sin and repented and were baptised. Their hearts and lives were changed.

WHAT DOES IT MEAN TODAY? Yeshua tells us in John 8:30-36 that all are slaves to sin but Yeshua has set us free. When we accept Yeshua, and His Ruach, He starts working with us to write His law/Torah on our hearts and to change our lives. Having His Torah written on our hearts makes us want to follow Him because we love Him, not because we have to or because we are scared not to.

WHAT CAN I DO? Have you asked Yeshua for His Ruach HaKodesh so you can have a new heart? If you haven't, what better time than today, the day we celebrate the giving of the Ruach? If you have already, this is a great day to ask for a refilling of the spirit and to think about what changes ADONAI has made in your life so far. Complete the activity to see what else you can do on Shavuot.

Reference

"The Festival of Shavuot arrived, and the believers all gathered in one place. Suddenly there came a sound from the sky like the roar of a violent wind and it filled the whole house where they were sitting. Then they saw what looked like tongues of fire, which separated and came to rest on each one of them. They were all filled with the Ruach HaKodesh and began to talk in different languages as the spirit enabled them to speak."
Acts 2:1-4 CJB

Reference

"You are to count seven weeks; you are to begin counting seven weeks from the time you first put your sickle to the standing grain. You are to observe the festival of Shavuot (weeks) for ADONAI your G-d with a voluntary offering, which you are to give in accordance to the decree ADONAI your G-d has prospered you. You are to rejoice in the presence of ADONAI your G-d...in the place where ADONAI your G-d will choose to have his name live. Remember that you were a slave in Egypt; then you will keep and obey these laws."
Deuteronomy 16:9-12
CJB

Night Vigil

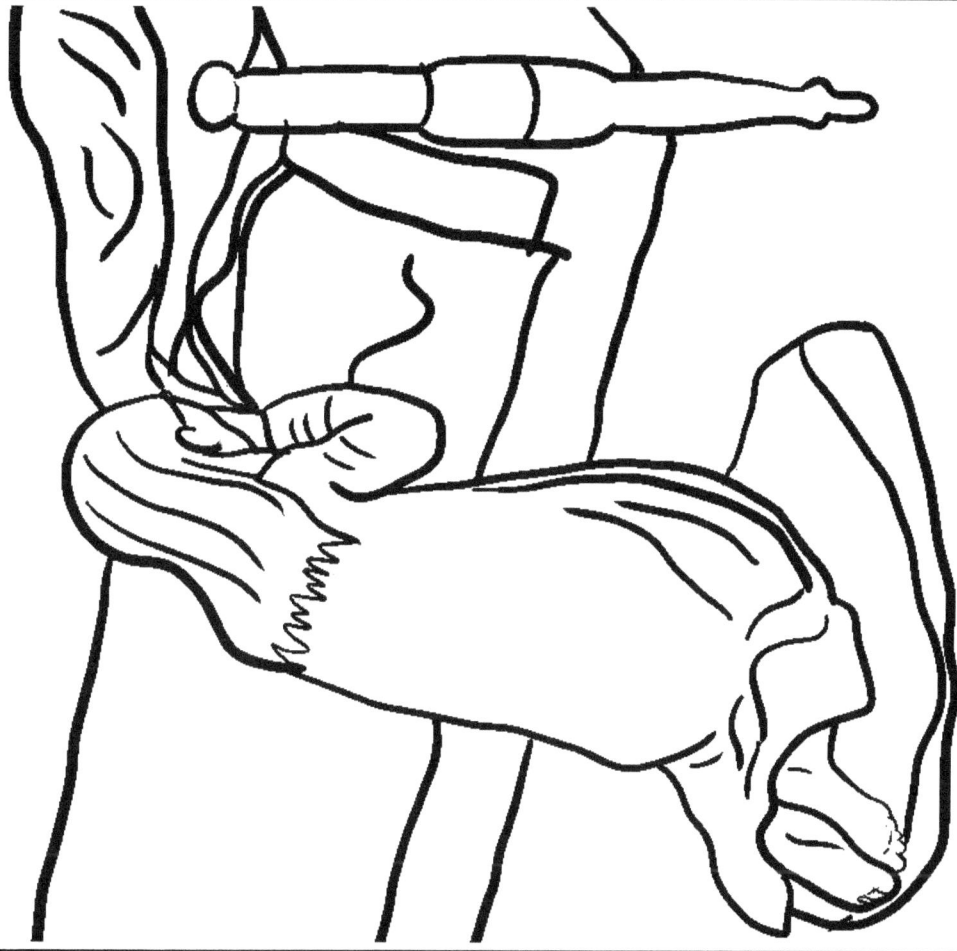

Shavout Activity Sheet

Here are some Ideas of what others do to celebrate Shavuot and what you might like to do. Match the words with the right pictures.

Candles

Charitable Giving

Stay up Late to Pray and Read the Torah

Decorate with Flowers

Make Nosh Snacks

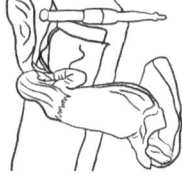

References and Websites Used

In order of Appearance

reformjudaism.org

Bible.org

Betemunah.org

Bibleprophecytruth.com

Wikimedia.org

Theworkofgodschildren.org

Richard Elofer

biblewheel.com

pecoc.co.za

Vintageprintable.com

wildbranch.org

Agapebiblestudy.com

Biblestudytools.com

biblehub.com

Bible.org

Torah.org

coolnotions.com

christianstackexchange.com

Jen Betham Lang-Live your Festival Heritage

itzikswell.blogspot.co.nz

abarim-publications.com

Discovertheword.org

Newlife.org

theblogofbaphomet.com

joshfeigelson.wordpress.com

preceptaustin.org

myjewishlearning.com

clal.org

lorettaoakes.blogspot.co.nz

Myredeemerlives.com

messianic-torah-truth-seeker.org

bible.ca

www.ingramcontent.com/pod-product-compliance
Lightning Source LLC
LaVergne TN
LVHW081449070426
835508LV00016B/1419